Look, I don't dance now

I make money moves

(ayy, ayy)

Say I don't

VOICES IN HIP-HOP / CARDI B

VOICES IN HIP-HOP

CARDI B

TREY CLARK

CREATIVE EDUCATION / CREATIVE PAPERBACKS

···Not too long
dancing for
··· (Eeoo
···Know it's rea
let you meet
··· (Eeoo

Published by Creative Education and Creative Paperbacks
P.O. Box 227, Mankato, Minnesota 56002
Creative Education and Creative Paperbacks are
imprints of The Creative Company
www.thecreativecompany.us

Design by Graham Morgan
Art direction by Blue Design (www.bluedes.com)

Images by Associated Press/Arthur Mola/Invision, cover, 3, 27; Getty Images/BRENDAN SMIALOWSKI, 41, Dia Dipasupil, 19, Emma McIntyre, 42, Frazer Harrison, 15, Gilbert Flores, 10, Jason Koerner, 9, 34, Jeff Kravitz, 24, 31, Kevin Winter, 36, Kevin Mazur, 45, Michael Hickey, 16, Rick Kern, 38, Rob Kim, 23, Roy Rochlin, 28, Steven Ferdman, 2; Wikimedia Commons/Atlantic Records, 22, Frank Schwichtenberg, 4, Gryffindor, 12
Every effort has been made to contact copyright holders for material reproduced in this book. Any omissions will be rectified in subsequent printings if notice is given to the publisher.

Library of Congress Cataloging-in-Publication Data
Names: Clark, Trey, author.
Title: Cardi B / by Trey Clark.
Description: Mankato, Minnesota : Creative Education and Creative Paperbacks, 2026. | Series: Voices in hip-hop | Includes index. | Audience: Ages 12–15 | Audience: Grades 7–9 | Summary: "Listen up! It's Cardi B, the wildly charismatic hip-hop artist. Part biography, part song lyric collection, this music-fueled title for high school readers celebrates the rapper's journey and voice. Includes a selected discography and index"– Provided by publisher.
Identifiers: LCCN 2024053908 (print) | LCCN 2024053909 (ebook) | ISBN 9798889892762 (library binding) | ISBN 9781682776421 (paperback) | ISBN 9798889893875 (ebook)
Subjects: LCSH: Cardi B, 1992– –Juvenile literature. | Rap musicians–United States–Biography–Juvenile literature.
Classification: LCC ML3930.C255 C53 2026 (print) | LCC ML3930.C255 (ebook) | DDC 782.421649092 [B]–dc23/eng/20241113
LC record available at https://lccn.loc.gov/2024053908
LC ebook record available at https://lccn.loc.gov/2

Printed in India

ago, I was
ollars

lly real if I
my mama

contents

Foreword

• • •

"She's so sweet. And she's so kind. And that's why I really like her cause she's real. Like, you know, you don't really run across a lot of raw people. Whatever come to her mind first, that's what she sayin', that's how she feels. So I never walk away like 'Did she mean that?' No, cause if she thought, she said it, and she meant it. So I absolutely love that about her."

—MEGAN THEE STALLION, *ENTERTAINMENT TONIGHT*, SEPTEMBER 19, 2023

Introduction

Not too long ago, I was dancing for dollars (Eeoow)
Know it's really real if I let you meet my mama (Eeoow)
You don't want a girl like me, I'm too crazy
But every other girl you meet is fugazi (Okurrrt)

—FROM "GIRLS LIKE YOU (FEAT. CARDI B)" ON MAROON 5'S ALBUM *RED PILL BLUES*, 2018

While it takes some hip-hop artists years to create a recognizable image, Cardi B came into the music industry with an already established persona. At times boisterous and at times humble, Cardi B's personality has been instrumental in making her one of the most impactful voices in hip-hop.

Cultivated through her social media presence and time on reality TV, the world fell in love with Cardi B for just how real she was in her music, and how it reflected her life. She can be flexing on her critics in one song by talking about her successes as in "Press." She can be vulnerable about her personal relationships in another song as in "Ring."

Additionally, Cardi B is resilient. Regardless of any drama she may find herself in, she stays true to herself and bounces back stronger than she was before. Her music reflects this "never give up" attitude. Setbacks only serve to show how she's become a better person as a result.

Cardi B made a strong impression when she first entered the music industry. She is the first U.S. female rapper to have multiple YouTube videos reach a billion views. She has several music awards, ranging from MTV Video Music Awards to a Grammy. She has acted in several movies and TV shows and helped produce TV shows. Even with so many accomplishments under her belt, she has yet to slow down in her career and continues to grow as a person through her music.

The Bronx, New York City

Early Family Life

Yo, some people know me as a stripper h—
But stripper h— get the money and blow digits though
A lot of b— talkin' down on me like I'm a joke
Talk s—, I'll f— your man, send him back hella broke

—FROM THE 2017 SINGLE "STRIPPER H—"

kurrr! Let's start from the beginning. Before Cardi B became one of the leading ladies in hip-hop, she was just Belcalis Marlenis Almánzar, a young girl born on October 11, 1992, and raised in The Bronx, New York. Her stage name Cardi B is based on a nickname, Bacardi. Her mother, Clara Almánzar, is from Trinidad. Her father, Carlos Almánzar, is from the Dominican Republic. They were married when Cardi's younger sister Hennessy was born in 1995, but they divorced in the early 2000s.

ardi B reminisced about her father in a 2018 *Rolling Stone* interview. She said that, while he was "the cool parent," he inspired her to "be so careful with my money and always try to invest" because she had seen "people who have it all and then lose it all." As she was growing up, the need for money, an interest in the performing arts, and her mother acted as her main motivators. After Cardi B performed the song "Bad Romance" by Lady Gaga in her high school talent show, her friends encouraged her to write her own, more explicit remixes of popular songs. She enjoyed making her friends laugh.

However, Cardi B's early life had just as many lows as highs. People body-shamed her for being slim and for her hair. In addition to her mother being strict, Cardi B developed a strong desire to be a version of herself that would command attention. She said during a 2021 conversation with Mariah Carey for *Interview* magazine: "I always wanted to be what my mom didn't let me . . . I think she didn't want me to grow up so fast, because the kids around my neighborhood grew up fast."

After high school, Cardi B was kicked out of her home at age 18 and attended community college. But she struggled to balance her classes and her job at a local deli. She told *Rolling Stone* that she "had to debate, 'Do I wanna go to class or do I wanna finish my shift?'"

The money she earned dancing helped her move on from a bad relationship and eventually buy a house. However, Cardi B remained uncomfortable about her dancing. She noted in an 2018 video for *Cosmopolitan* with Naomi Smalls: "When my mom found out I was a dancer, she was pretty upset . . . Knowing that she used to hate it, it didn't allow me to get comfortable with what I was doing."

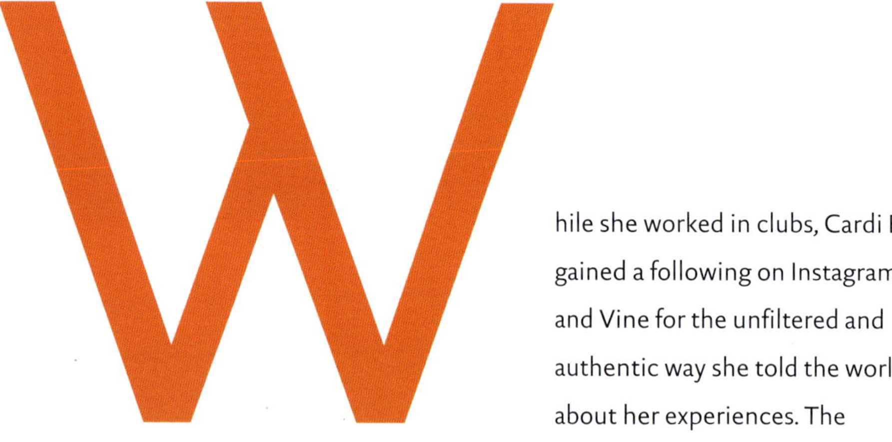

While she worked in clubs, Cardi B gained a following on Instagram and Vine for the unfiltered and authentic way she told the world about her experiences. The popularity she gained in social media catapulted her into starring on the reality show *Love & Hip Hop: New York* in 2015. During the same year, Cardi B made her musical debut on Shaggy's song "Boom Boom (Remix)." She created a mixtape a year later.

LOVE & HIP-HOP

Love & Hip Hop is a series of TV shows that documents the lives of important people in the music industry, specifically in hip-hop and rhythm and blues (R&B). While originally starting in New York City, the series is also based in Miami, Florida; Atlanta, Georgia; and Hollywood, California. The series has been seen as controversial due to seeming unrealistic at times, but it still receives very high ratings in spite of its critics. Additionally, the series has acted as a launch pad for the careers of artists like Cardi B and K. Michelle.

I'm just into
making
money,
I ain't into
making love
When you

Mixtapes and TV

hen she looked back on her early days, Cardi B told *Rolling Stone* that her haters were "expecting me to drop something trash. It just made me, like, 'Aha, I gotta study these other rappers . . . Study how to do something different from them. You know all these female rappers, they talking about they money, they talking about they cars, so it's like, what's something that I enjoy? I enjoy fights!"

Her time on *Love & Hip Hop* seasons six and seven only emphasized her confrontational and endearing personality. It seemed that she found the perfect style of rap for herself when she dropped her first mixtape in 2016 and created a second mixtape in 2017.

Cardi B left *Love & Hip Hop* after season seven to pursue her music career. In 2017, she collaborated with Atlanta rapper Offset and his trio Migos on "Motorsport" and "Lick (Remix)." But her greatest success at the time occurred after she signed to Atlantic Records.

She released her first single, "Bodak Yellow," to significant success. It reached the number-one spot on the Billboard Hot 100 and earned Cardi B her first Grammy nominations for Best Rap Performance and Best Rap Song in 2018.

SUCCESS THROUGH ATLANTIC RECORDS

Atlantic Records is a record label founded in 1947. Artists like Aretha Franklin, Ray Charles, Bruno Mars, Led Zeppelin, and Wiz Khalifa were signed to Atlantic Records, and all have experienced tremendous success as a result. Atlantic Records promoted Cardi B's music to the public through marketing campaigns and using their connections in the industry to have her music played on radio stations.

Look, I don't dance now
I make money moves (ayy, ayy)
Say I don't gotta dance
I make money move

—FROM "BODAK YELLOW" ON THE 2018 ALBUM *INVASION OF PRIVACY*

Early Growth

Cardi B has undoubtedly changed over the years since her first mixtapes. The main difference in Cardi B's music from her first feature to her breakout single was presentation. Personality-wise, she was always funny, kind, and ready for action, but it took time for her to learn how to express it through her music.

She had to study other female rappers to figure out what style she fit into, and she drew inspiration from a variety of sources. As a person who grew up listening to reggae, Spanish, and older hip-hop artists like Missy Elliot and Ja Rule, Cardi B combined some very different genres of music, creating the image she wanted to project.

She survived when she had to, and she translated her success on the club scene into a musical career. She proudly claimed her past as a dancer and used that experience in much of her early catalog. Though she continued to reference her past in her works, she shifted away from talking about it too frequently. When "Bodak Yellow" was released, it cemented Cardi B's image as a confident musician and public figure.

'Bodak Yellow'

I nspired by rapper Kodak Black's 2015 song "No Flockin," "Bodak Yellow" was Cardi B's first single on the Billboard Hot 100. She was the first artist of Dominican descent to reach it since the chart's creation.

"Bodak Yellow" pushed Cardi B onto the hip-hop scene with force. She still flaunted her trademark fighting themes, but she also leaned more into the image of a wealthy woman paying homage to her fellow artists. The song also kicked off Cardi B's struggle with public perception. Some people saw "Bodak Yellow" as a clone of "No Flockin." Cardi B did not engage with these critics and allowed her success to speak for itself.

Cardi B performs in Toronto, Canada, in 2017.

VOICES IN HIP-HOP

In a 2018 interview with iHeartRadio, Cardi B said: "The weirdest and most annoying thing that I gained from fame is just people pressuring you. I feel like I don't have any privacy. I don't even know who to trust around me anymore because there's always a story around me, and it's just like, who's saying these type of things? I also don't like how there's people that never even met me, that's always commenting about me. They're saying mean things about me, or they just make an assumption of the type of person that I am, and they don't even know me."

All of that talk and I'm calling it out
Public opinions from private accounts
You not a check, then you gotta bounce

—FROM "CLOUT (FEAT. CARDI B)" ON OFFSET'S 2019 ALBUM *FATHER OF 4*

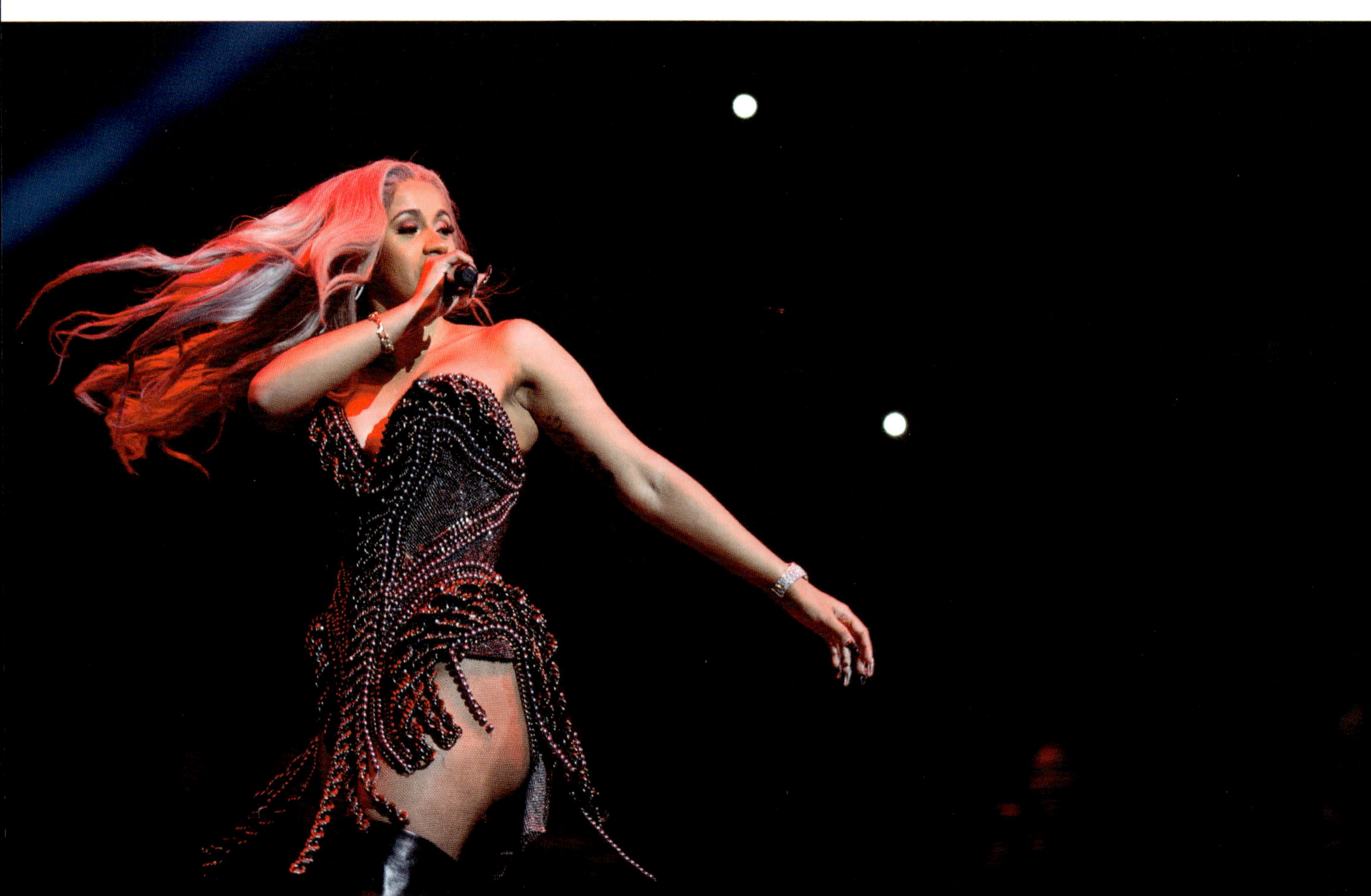

Marriage

• • •

Cardi B said in an interview that she and Offset "polish each other." She added: "I could always ask him, 'Do you think this is OK to do? Do you think I'm getting tricked?'"

—2017 ***ROLLING STONE***

Cardi B and Offset started dating in early 2017. The couple secretly married in September 2017—in fact, before Offset publicly proposed to Cardi B at a concert in Philadelphia that October.

Rumors soon swirled around Offset and Cardi B's marriage, and they picked up steam due to news coverage. In a single week, rumors spread that the couple had broken up and come back together. Additionally, people from Cardi B's past accused her of hurting them, she debunked pregnancy rumors, and she addressed allegations about Offset cheating on her with other women.

The pressures of stardom fell heavily upon her, but she handled it the way she always had: honestly. In April 2018, she revealed that she was pregnant with the couple's daughter Kulture (who was born that July). Cardi B and Offset also shared the front cover of the June 2018 *Rolling Stone* magazine. Despite the controversies surrounding the marriage, Cardi B pushed forward and followed up "Bodak Yellow" with her first ever album.

Now I like dollars, I like diamonds
I like stunting, I like shining
I like million dollar deals
Where's my pen? B— I'm signin'

—FROM "I LIKE IT" ON THE 2018 ALBUM *INVASION OF PRIVACY*

Offset and Cardi B

The First Album

• • •

Cardi B's first album, aptly named *Invasion of Privacy,* was the culmination of five years of experience in the music industry at that time. Released in 2018, *Invasion of Privacy* had two singles reach number one on the Billboard Hot 100, "Bodak Yellow" and "I Like It." The album consisted of features from Migos, Chance the Rapper, Kehlani, YG, and other notable artists.

It had more traditional songs from Cardi B, like "Drip," that showed her flaunting her status and wealth. Slower songs, like "Ring," showed the rapper's more sensitive side which rarely appeared in her music. In addition, "I Like It" placed Cardi B's

Press, press, press, press, press
Cardi don't need more press
Kill 'em all, put them h— to rest

—FROM THE 2019 SINGLE "PRESS"

Trinidadian and Dominican heritage at the forefront, with a music video that accentuated the way her culture inspired her music. In the song and video, Cardi B teamed up with J Balvin and Bad Bunny, who rapped in Spanish.

In an interview with iHeartRadio the day her album dropped, Cardi B said: "The message that I have for the haters and people that doubt me, and people that think I'm not gonna win, I just want to tell you this: The more you hate, the more I want to prove things to you, and the more I prove things to you, it makes me feel good. Y'all give me the power because if everybody loves me and if everybody keep telling me that you winning, I would feel like I don't have to work so hard. So, when a hater talks bad about me, I feel like I gotta keep proving things to them. So, it makes me want to work harder . . . and that's why I be winning. Thank you."

Stacking Successes

Am I your lover or I'm just your vice? (Woo, yeah, yeah)
A little crazy, but I'm just your type (Okurr)
You want the lips and the curves, need the whips and the furs
And the diamonds I prefer, and my closet his and hers, ayy

—FROM THE 2019 SINGLE "SOUTH OF THE BORDER"

fter the release of *Invasion of Privacy*, Cardi B showed no sign of stopping in 2018 and 2019. She released songs such as "Press" and "Money" and appeared more frequently in features on the songs of other artists. "Finesse (Remix),"

that I want to spoil my child for the rest of my life. And in order for me to spoil my child for the rest of my life, I have to have money, and make money for the rest of my life."

The interview also touched on Cardi B's disdain for then-president Donald Trump, a question she would ask if invited to the White House, and what law she would create if she had the power to do so. When asked why she used her social media to speak about politics, Cardi B said: "Just living in my neighborhood made me always want to speak up always. Seeing the injustice. Seeing how kids my age, my color darker, were getting treated in my neighborhood. That always made me wanna be involved, even when I was a teenager." The year ended quietly for Cardi B in terms of music, but 2020 showed that she was still the same raunchy and unapologetic Grammy winner.

Out in public, make a scene
I don't cook, I don't clean
But let me tell you how I got this ring (ayy, ayy)

—FROM THE 2020 SINGLE "WAP"

'WAP'

Cardi B started off 2020 with a bang. She released "WAP" with Megan Thee Stallion and split public opinion about herself once again. With "WAP" reaching number one on the Billboard Hot 100, making it Cardi B's fourth number one, she dealt with people telling her that she should not be rapping so explicitly. Others enthusiastically supported "WAP" precisely because it was explicit, arguing that it was an empowering song due to its unapologetic expression of desire.

In a December 2020 article in *Billboard,* Julie Greenwald, a CEO of Atlantic Records, said: "Cardi's entire evolution has been driven by a singular, unswerving vision she has for herself—who she wants to be, what she wants to accomplish, and where she wants to be at every point in her career . . . There was no question that her talent, her charisma, and her determination would make her a musical and cultural icon."

You know tha
it's hittin', yo
know what
it's givin'

Hair, nails,
polar bear

Cardi B had her own YouTube show called *Cardi Tries* and had a one-on-one conversation with then-president elect Joe Biden through *Elle*. The COVID pandemic affected her similarly to the rest of the world. In her talk with Biden, she said: "I don't want to be lied to. We're dealing with a pandemic now, right? I just want answers. I wanna know when this is over. I wanna go back to my job. I wanna be able to go outside. I wanna be able to feel like I'm not trapped in my home."

Cardi B at a rally for Democratic presidential candidate Kamala Harris in Milwaukee, Wisconsin, in 2024

Up and Offset

Cardi B gave her fans a scare when her marriage had trouble once again in late 2020. She said that she had officially divorced Offset, but later retracted the statement. On top of the release in 2021of her song "Up," which became her fifth number one on the Billboard Hot 100, she announced that she was having another baby with Offset. Their son Wave was born that September.

Now with two children, Cardi B noticeably stepped back from music. "Up" was the only single she released for the entire year. Over the next two years, she released more singles, but she did not capture the same power that had pushed her to the number one spot on Billboard's Hot 100. When asked about her second album in a 2022 interview with *The Breakfast Club,* Cardi B said: "I have like a couple of songs that are like definite, I don't know. I don't know what's going on with me. I need to just make up my mind and put it out."

Other business ventures, like her alcoholic whipped cream Whipshots, pulled her away from music. Her statements reveal her business ambition. In a 2022 interview with *Complex* about Whipshots, Cardi B said: "I feel like if it was just mediocre, people would just be like, 'ah, whatever.' Things are always going to sell when you have hardcore fans, but I wanted this to be big. Like, bigger than life, and that is always the goal." Cardi B also sued a YouTuber for libel—broadcasting statements harmful to her reputation. She won the lawsuit and was awarded nearly $4 million in damages and legal fees.

You know that it's hittin', you know what it's givin'
Hair, nails, polar bear
I can survive in the coldest conditions

—FROM THE 2024 SINGLE "ENOUGH (MIAMI)"

2024 and Beyond

Unfortunately, the end of 2023 marked the "official" end of Cardi B and Offset's marriage—at least for the time being. Cardi B said in an Instagram Live: "I've been single for a minute now but afraid to like—not afraid, I just don't know how to tell the world." The couple appeared to be on good terms in 2024. Notably, Offset directed Cardi B's music video when she released her newest single "Enough (Miami)" in March.

Cardi B continued to be on good terms with Offset and the two did reconcile, but they went through another breakup in August 2024. The divorce proceedings were filed after the announcement of Cardi B's pregnancy with the couple's third child. The baby was born in September 2024.

With so much having already happened in Cardi B's life, where does she go from here? Cardi B has hinted at releasing another album, and she brings the same energy to her new ventures as she has had since "Bodak Yellow." She remains outspoken about her life and the issues she cares about. She is able to express herself in sincere and genuine ways. Her fans, haters, and biggest critics all come back to Cardi B because she is true to herself.

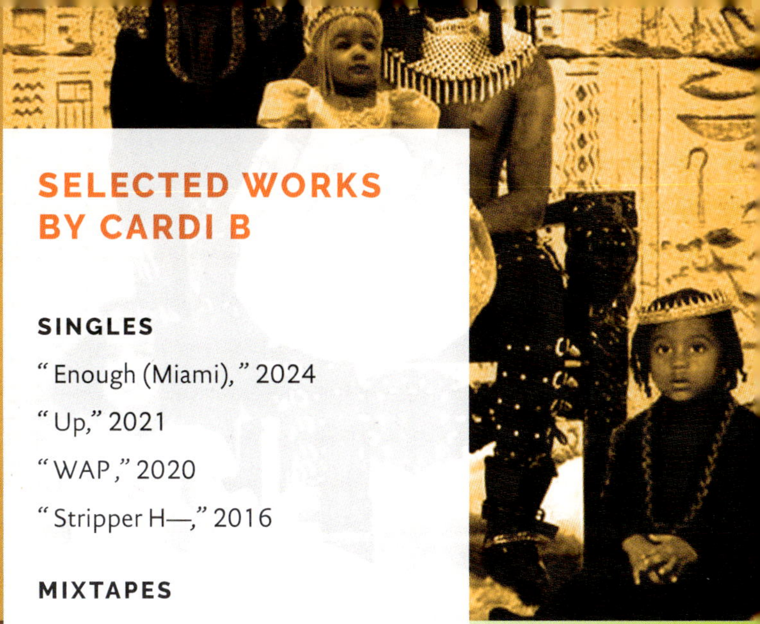

SELECTED WORKS BY CARDI B

SINGLES

"Enough (Miami)," 2024

"Up," 2021

"WAP," 2020

"Stripper H—," 2016

MIXTAPES

Gangsta B— Music, Vol. 1, 2016

FEATURES (SINGLES)

"South of the Border," 2019

"Girls Like You," 2018

FEATURES (ALBUMS)

Father of 4, 2019

Red Pill Blues, 2018

STUDIO ALBUMS

Invasion of Privacy, 2019

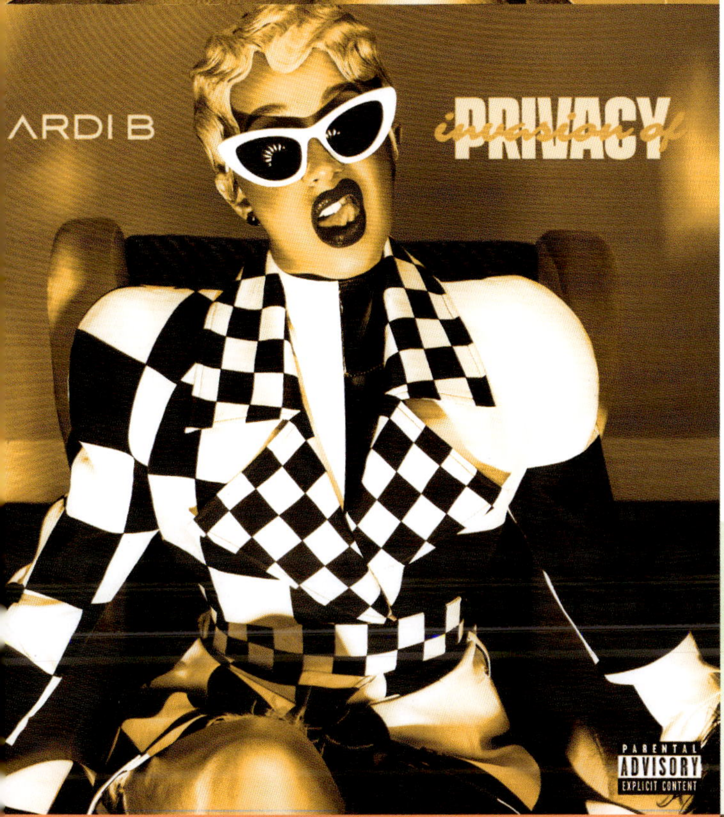

INDEX